IMAGES
of England

MONKSEATON
AND HILLHEADS

The earliest record of Hill Heads Farm is in 1757. In this picture, dating to the early 1900s, it seems that the group of men sitting around the fence have gathered to play a game of quoits, which has always been a popular game in the area. The farmer at this time was Thomas Thompson, who is sitting in the centre of the picture, holding a stick. Thomas was well-known in the area and was often referred to as the Grand Old Man, or Father of Whitley, because of his long service on the local council, as well as his involvement with many other local institutions.

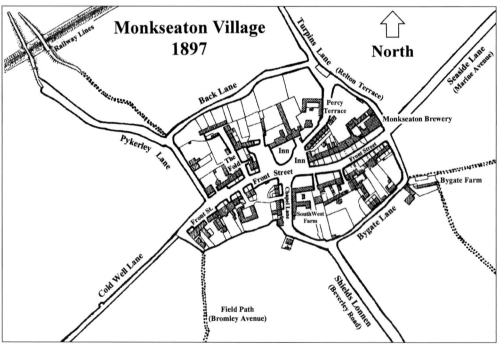

A map of Monkseaton Village, 1897.

IMAGES
of England

MONKSEATON
AND HILLHEADS

Compiled by
Charles W. Steel

TEMPUS

First published 2000
Copyright © Charles W. Steel, 2000

Tempus Publishing Limited
The Mill, Brimscombe Port,
Stroud, Gloucestershire, GL5 2QG

ISBN 0 7524 2064 X

Typesetting and origination by
Tempus Publishing Limited
Printed in Great Britain by
Midway Clark Printing, Wiltshire

Mission House, Monkseaton.

Originally the turnip house for Monkseaton Village Farm, this building was purchased in 1899 by a Col. T.W. Elliott, who converted it into a little church for use by the Anglicans. In 1913, the Anglicans vacated the building and the Wesleyans from nearby Chapel Lane took over the building, which continued in use as a Methodist church. The two cannons outside, originally part of the ordinances of Scarborough Castle, were presented at the opening of the church, by Col. Elliott. They remained outside the church until 1942, when they were removed in a salvage drive, to be melted down for materials during the Second World War.

For many years, the building was known as 'The Gun Chapel', and despite the many changes that have taken place over the years, the church, which is still in use today, is easily recognisable.

Contents

Acknowledgements

Contributors include:

Mrs Connie Adamson, Monkseaton.
Mr John Ewan, West Monkseaton.
Mr Paul Samuel, The Beehive Inn, Earsdon.
Mrs G. Scott, Monkseaton.
Mrs Elizabeth Steel, Monkseaton.
Mr John R. Steel, Leeds.

I am also grateful for the assistance of the staff of North Shields Local Studies Centre, and finally, special thanks go to John Alexander for his advice and encouragement.

The Black Horse Inn, originally built in 1793 as a two storey building. It was later remodelled to include a third floor. This picture was taken in 1936, shortly before it was demolished. The little shop to the left, originally Scott & Robsons' grocery store was taken over by George W. Haimes, whose sign on the front is now apparent.

Introduction

Although the village of Monkseaton has a long and historic past and information is available and accessible, old photographs and pictures seem to be scarce, and very little seems to have been written about the area. In 1893, a local historian called William Weaver Tomlinson wrote a book entitled 'Cullercoats, Whitley and Monkseaton', which contains an interesting factual history of the area during the latter part of the 1800s. As nothing appears to have been published since that time relating to the Monkseaton area, the book itself has been an invaluable source of reference to help put together some of the material required for the preparation of this one.

Despite the fact that over the past eighty years, Monkseaton Village has been absorbed into the urban confines of the nearby town of Whitley Bay, its history pre-dates that town by many years, and to anyone who resides in Monkseaton, the place is still referred to as 'The Village'. Over the years, many changes have taken place, most of which have been so gradual that they have simply passed by unnoticed. Many of the old farms and buildings that once stood in Monkseaton Village have long since disappeared and remain only as distant memories. The rest sadly, have long since been forgotten.

Monkseaton dates back to at least the twelfth century, when it was simply known as 'Seton'. This is probably a derivative of the words 'sea' and 'tun', i.e.: the village being near to the sea, and a 'tun', meaning a hill or rise. When King Henry I granted lands to the Prior of Tynemouth around 1106, the name was altered to 'Seton Monachorum'. The prefix 'Monk' is often found in connection with places belonging to religious houses, and so in this case it became known as Monk Seaton, or Seaton of the Monks.

From the thirteenth to the eighteenth century there are frequent references, monastic and civil, relating to the farms and dwellings, and some names mentioned are of local interest, perhaps the most noticeable of which is that of the Mills family. Thomas Mills held farms in the area, and in 1688 resided in the farmhouse, which stood on the site of the Ship Inn. His grandson, also called Thomas, died at his house in Monkseaton on 18 November 1775, having been the curate of Jarrow with Heworth.

Of the village itself, little can be recorded other than by historical references, but it would appear that judging by the standards of those bygone days, it was a place of some importance. From the year 1577, coal was worked on the land of the Village Farm. In the seventeenth, eighteenth and nineteenth centuries there were several farms, as well as there being the usual trades people, such as blacksmiths, shoemakers and shopkeepers.

There was a brewery, and with 3 or more inns, the population which varied between 427 in 1801, rising to 952 by the year 1901, was well catered for with ale!

It is of interest to note how the historians of earlier years summed up their view of the village:

1811: 'Monkseaton is a pleasant village, situated 3½ miles north-west by north from Tynemouth to which parish it belongs, and contains some well built houses belonging to different gentlemen and farmers. Here are also three Public Houses and one Brewery'.

1825: 'Monkseaton is a pleasant village, situated 3½ miles north-west by north from Tynemouth. It contains five Farmholds, a Methodist Meeting House, two Public Houses and a large Brewery belonging to Messrs. Dryden & Co.'

1841 'Monkseaton is an irregularly built village of no trade, with the exception of a respectable Brewery belonging to Messrs. Sinclair & Co'.

1853: 'As I approached the pretty little whitewashed village of Monkseaton from the west side, it was pleasing to hear the incessant tapping of the hammers of the local tinkers. At close hand the people of the place were disappointing. The tinkers were industrious only by fits and starts and did not look upon the village as their particular or cherished abode. They treated it as a sort of workshop and spent much of their time wandering the country, selling their wares and carousing'.

1893: 'Monkseaton is a pretty little village, formerly the sea town of the monks of Tynemouth. When its garden trees are in full leaf, the village has a very picturesque appearance, situated as it is, on a very slight eminence, and many visitors who wish to combine some of the charms of the country with those of the seaside, patronise it during the summer months'.

1907: 'We recommend Monkseaton, with a walk to the shore before noon, and a rest after lunch, with a country stroll in the evening. To many people, the rural situation, a little from the Links with the slightly elevated position, forms a strong attraction. Monkseaton Village itself is chiefly of good new houses, but there is sufficient of the old characteristic to make the place interesting as it is quiet and beautiful. Much has been done in the use of foliage to make the district attractive and it is rapidly becoming a charming and popular resort and the chief residential suburb of Newcastle upon Tyne, for such it would seem nature has destined it'.

Sadly, since these colourful descriptions were written the farms have gradually disappeared, and have been replaced with business premises, houses and shops. Housing estates now cover the many fields that were once dotted with wells and water pumps. Trees and hedgerows have been uprooted and cleared to accommodate new and wider roads, and a car park has replaced what was once the village green. The village is today a very different place from what was once 'Seton Monachorum' – 'The Seaton of the Monks'.

The areas that skirt the outer boundary of Monkseaton to the southeast, are Hillheads (formerly known as Whitley Hill Heads), along with the villages of New York and Murton to the south-west, and Earsdon to the north. Although these villages have now been incorporated into the suburbs of neighbouring Whitley Bay and North Shields, they are still considered by the local residents as villages in their own right, all of which have their unique story to tell.

This book therefore, might bring back some memories to the older folk that remember Monkseaton and the nearby villages as they used to be; and for the younger generation it will hopefully serve to show a little about how the area looked in days gone by.

Charles W. Steel
Summer 2000

One
Monkseaton Village

An aerial view of Monkseaton Village, 1986.

Monkseaton Village around 1912. The original Ship Inn is on the left; the house next to it is East Farm, then Scott & Robsons' grocery store, and of course on the far right hand side, is the old Black Horse Inn.

There was no traffic on the road in 1909 to bother the horse or trap driver, who seem quite content to wait patiently near the brewery in the middle of Front Street. The distant building is Monkseaton Railway Station, and the large double dormer house is now known as 'The Lawns' rest home. The house next to it, (which appears closer than it actually is) is at the end of Kensington Gardens.

In order to reach Monkseaton from Whitley Village, it was necessary to follow a pretty country path through the fields and cross over the railway lines, which led to the eastern edge of what was referred to as 'Fancy Fields'. Continuing across the lines, the pathway then ran between two gates into the south-east corner of Monkseaton Village. This illustration by Thomas Eyre Macklin, dated 1893, shows 'Fancy Fields', viewed from a point at the present St Ronans Road junction with Marmion Terrace. The houses in the background are on Front Street, and the prominent building with its tall chimney is Monkseaton Brewery.

T.S. Hutton was a local artist who painted this picture of 'Fancy Fields', Monkseaton, dated 1892. This view looks west towards Monkseaton Village, from a point which is now occupied by the buildings, on the north side of St Ronans Road, near Waverley Avenue. As in the previous illustration, Front Street and Monkseaton Brewery can be seen to the right, with Bygate Farm and Bygate Road visible at the end of the path towards the left.

Bromley Place, (now Bromley Avenue) 1951. Cauldwell Lane runs from left to right in the foreground. The houses in the picture were later demolished in order to make way for a car showroom.

An aerial view of Cauldwell Lane at the junction with Pykerley Road, taken from the site of Homeprior House during its construction in 1986.

Wilsons Garage, Cauldwell Lane, 1982.

A muddy Vernon Drive in 1936. Monkseaton County Secondary School, seen here, was built in 1932, followed by a number of houses, directly opposite. The road was not properly laid out until some years later, and then adopted by the council in 1957.

The car parked outside the boys' entrance of Monkseaton County Secondary School in 1936 seems to be causing some interest.

This 1893 sketch by Thomas Eyre Macklin shows the west-end of Front Street, with the edge of the Fold visible towards the right. The view looks west towards Cold Well Lane (now known as Cauldwell Lane). The name Cold Well, was derived from a well situated in a field next to Front Street and Pykerley Lane (or Pykerley Road as it is now known). The well was provided with water from a natural supply which ran from the top of Cold Well Lane, and followed the course of the present road, into Monkseaton Village and past the front of Percy Terrace. Water was tapped from here to supply the reservoirs for Monkseaton Brewery, situated in the rear gardens of Monkseaton House.

Front Street, Monkseaton, looking west, in 1916. 'West House', part of West Farm, is the large building in the background towards the left of the picture, and next to it are whitewashed cottages which formed part of 'The Fold'. These buildings were later replaced with a row of shops, flats and an office block. The two larger houses on the right, built in 1814, stood near the end of Roseberry Terrace, and were called 'Murie House' and 'Jessamine House'. Prior to this time, an old inn called the Seven Stars occupied the site.

Front Street, Monkseaton, looking east in 1905. The white cottages to the left form part of 'The Fold', and to the right, Nos 47 to 51 Front Street still remain today, beyond which the tall roof of the Black Horse Inn is visible.

A crowd gathers for the opening ceremony of Monkseaton Methodist church, Front Street, on 12 May 1913. Alderman John Robert Hogg, JP, is near the centre of the picture, accepting the keys on behalf of the Wesleyans, from Col. T.W. Elliott, (third from the right).

An interior view of Monkseaton Methodist church in 1913.

Chapel Lane was named after the old Wesleyan chapel that stood on the south side of the road, opposite the rear of Southwest Farm. The chapel shown on the extreme left, was built in 1843 by the village grocer, shoemaker, blacksmith and two labourers. In 1890 some restoration work was carried out, and a porch was added. In 1913, when the Wesleyans left to take over the chapel on Front Street, this building was sold to a Mr Henry B. Saint, who dedicated it to the Congregationalists. The chapel later became known as Fairway Hall, and was used for general purposes. Then on the 29 August 1940, the chapel was destroyed in an air raid, and was replaced by a builders' yard and glass store. A blacksmith's shop stood just beyond the chapel, followed by Rose Cottage, which was at one time an inn called the Three Horse Shoes Inn.

A smartly dressed group of children and parents proudly display their Sunday school banner, as they pose for the photographer at the door of the Wesleyan church, Chapel Lane, in 1912.

Monkseaton Cottage and Monkseaton House in 1950. Monkseaton Cottage is probably the oldest surviving building in the village, as it was built during the 1400s as a farm byre, prior to its eventual conversion to a dwelling house. During the late 1800s, it was the home of Col. T.W. Elliott, a local benefactor of the Anglican chapel which stood opposite the cottage. The larger building next door is Monkseaton House, built in 1806 as the residence of a Dr Roxby. During the mid 1800s, it became the residence of William Davison, who built two reservoirs in the rear garden to supply water for Monkseaton Brewery, which he owned. Both buildings still exist, and are now residential care homes.

Coronation Row cottages, stood on Front Street, directly opposite the Wesleyan church, from where this picture was taken in 1934. Dryden & Co., owners of Monkseaton Brewery at that time, originally built the cottages in 1821 to house the brewery workers. The cottages were typical of their time, having outside whitewashed walls, with doors and shutters painted black in white painted frames; the floors were flagged and made of brick. The cottages probably took their name from the coronation of George IV in 1820. They were demolished in 1936 to accommodate the building of the new Black Horse Inn.

The middle cottage of Coronation Row was called 'Comfy Home', and was for many years the residence of a Sally Smith, who made a living by making and selling home-made sweets, during the 1860s. This picture dates to 1935, just prior to its demolition.

Coronation Row Cottages, under demolition during 1936. The Black Horse Inn which can be seen in the background, was demolished soon afterwards, and rebuilt on the same site.

The village blacksmith, Joe Davidson is seen here shoeing a horse at his smithy, situated in The Fold, Monkseaton during the 1920s. The identity of the man on the left is unknown.

Nos 1, 3 and 5 The Fold, stood at the junction with Front Street, Monkseaton. This picture was taken in 1955 shortly before demolition work began. The houses were replaced with a small office block. The derelict land in the centre later became sheltered housing.

This house which stood between Roseberry Terrace and The Fold, faced onto Front Street. It was destroyed by a bomb during an air raid on 29 August 1940.

The Fold, Monkseaton, 1986.

Front Street, looking west from the Black Horse Inn, around 1916.

Front Street, looking west, around 1915. This view, taken from the corner of the Black Horse Inn, shows Chapel Lane, and what is believed to be the old village slaughter house, to the immediate left. The gable end of the house beyond, is No. 47 Front Street. West House, on the corner of Pykerley Lane, is visible to the right.

Looking west up Bygate Road in 1956. The stone built house, called 'Rock Cottage', was built in 1790 to form part of Bygate Farm. From 1821, John and Ann Dunn resided here, and a stone plaque above the front door referred to the fact that the couple were in residence at this house whilst alterations were effected during this year. The plaque shows the initials of John and Ann Dunn, followed by the date 1821. This stone was sometimes referred to as a 'Wedding Stone' and was for many years pointed out to tourists. John Dunn married his second wife, Ann Hutchinson, on 8 April 1805 – sixteen years prior to the stone being affixed above the door. When Rock Cottage was demolished in 1965, the Wedding Stone was removed, and was retained by the then owners, Mr and Mrs C.P, Scott, of Clayton House, Monkseaton. Rock Cottage was later replaced with a new building called Rockville Bungalow.

A frontal view of Rock Cottage during the 1950s.

The Wedding Stone, with the initials of John and Ann Dunn, displayed above the doorway of Rock Cottage.

Demolition work starts on Rock Cottage in 1965.

This small stone building, called Garden Cottage is situated on Bygate Road, and over the years has been extensively modernised. During the 1840s it was romantically known as 'Ramsay's Fort' because the owner, Robert Ramsay, was supposed to have placed two imitation cannons on the roof, pointing along Shields Lonnen (Beverley Road), with the intention of 'frightening away the French', should they ever decide to invade the area! This photograph is dated 1930.

This is Lynn Cottage, another old house which stood on Bygate Road, opposite Bygate Farm.

Lynn Cottage underwent major refurbishment and renovation in 1961, the extent of which can be compared to the previous photograph. The cottage still remains today.

Thomas Johnson is standing in the doorway, and along with his daughter, Dorothy Jane Johnson, they ran this confectionery shop at No. 4 St Ronans Road, Monkseaton, from 1913 to 1934. Their residence was nearby, at No. 49 Melrose Avenue. This photograph was taken during the 1920s. The shop has long gone, and has since been converted into a private residence.

Adams Series. The Gardens Monkseaton. 251.

The girl on the tricycle seems to be showing the photographer some interest as she poses for this picture taken next to No. 23 The Gardens, in 1920. (Note the tall chimney of Monkseaton Brewery in the background).

Monkseaton Infants School, Chapel Lane, in 1952. The boys, probably pupils from the school, seem to be having fun walking along the stone wall of South West Farm. Chapel Lane was widened during this year, and the wall was demolished and rebuilt further to the left.

Rose Cottage stood on Chapel Lane, not far from the junction with Front Street. This view is dated 1900, but the building itself dates from 1795 when it opened as an ale house under the name of the Seven Stars. Over the years, this building has undergone many changes and alterations, having been an inn, a shop, a post office, a builders office, and latterly, a private residence, which was often referred to as 'Garnicks Cottage', after the last resident. The building was demolished in 1998 to be replaced by a new house.

On 9 July 1927, a large crowd gathered at the junction of Percy Terrace and Relton Terrace for the presentation ceremony of a stone trough, by the Metropolitan Drinking Fountain and Cattle Trough Association, to Whitley & Monkseaton Urban District Council. The trough, which still remains in situ, is now used for ornamental flower displays.

Percy Terrace, Monkseaton, around 1935. The stone wall on the left was the rear section of Monkseaton Brewery, and the visible houses are Nos 1 and 2 Percy Terrace.

The terraced houses on the right are numbered 2 to 12 Kenilworth Road. This view, taken during the 1920s, looks south towards St Ronans Road.

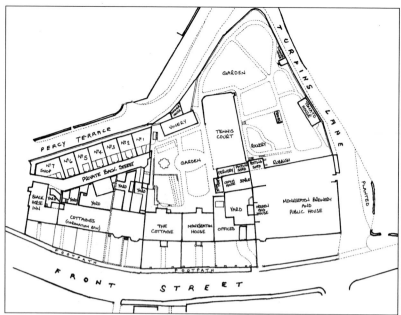

This plan of Monkseaton is dated 1877, and shows the centre of the village, with the land and buildings that stood between Front Street and Percy Terrace.

This scene of Front Street is believed to have been painted around 1887, by a local artist called Edith F. Grey, who was a resident in Monkseaton during that year. Monkseaton Brewery can be seen to the right, and behind the tree is the gable end of Monkseaton House. As there were no recognised footpaths in Monkseaton Village at this time, Front Street was nothing more than a farm track with a wall and a gate at each end. The nearby divergent road became 'Bye Gate', which may have some bearing on the name of the street running parallel with it – Bygate Road. It is quite probable that at one time, even as a cart track, Bygate Road was once the main street through Monkseaton. The gates were removed around 1845, and although this picture was painted some years later, the scene shows how Front Street would have looked at that time.

30

Front Street, Monkseaton, around 1920. Now the main street through the village, the visible buildings, from right to left, are: Monkseaton Wesleyan church; Village Farm House, a small whitewashed cottage, once used by the village blacksmith, (this building stood on the site of what is now a DIY shop); Ivy Cottage; Lily Cottage (demolished to make way for Alder Court); Gourd Cottage; Clayton House, and finally a row of brick built cottages which have now been converted into a row of shops.

Clayton House, (No. 21 Front Street, Monkseaton), around 1960.

A view of the rear of Clayton House around 1960. When Clayton House was first built, it may originally have faced onto Bygate Road, as the rear section of the house, in Georgian style, is older than the frontal section which is in Victorian Style.

The lime washed building in the centre of the picture shows Lily Cottage, with Ivy Cottage to its right. The edge of Gourd Cottage is just visible to the extreme left, now used by the Quakers, and better known today as the Friends Meeting House.

This 1961 view, taken from Alder Court, shows the old houses in Roseberry Terrace. Many people will remember the white house at the end of the row as Taylor's Fish & Chip Shop.

Christopher P. Scott was the son of Christopher and Margaret Scott, who ran Scott and Robsons grocery shop, at the top of Percy Terrace. He was also the local chimney sweep and drain clearance expert, running the business from his residence at Clayton House. With his fleet of bicycles, he is posing in the foreground for this photograph, along with two employees in 1958.

The name of the artist remains a mystery, but this old painting of the Black Horse Inn, with Coronation Row cottages, and the Monkseaton Brewery chimney visible behind, shows how the village would have looked around the early 1800s. The old Ship Inn is visible on the extreme left, and the little shop in between, still remains to this day. The haystacks in the distance belong to Village Farm, and are standing on the site of the present railway station.

John Falconer Slater was a well-known local artist, who painted many views of the Whitley, Cullercoats and Tynemouth areas. This picture, painted by him in 1925, shows a tranquil scene in the middle of Monkseaton Village.

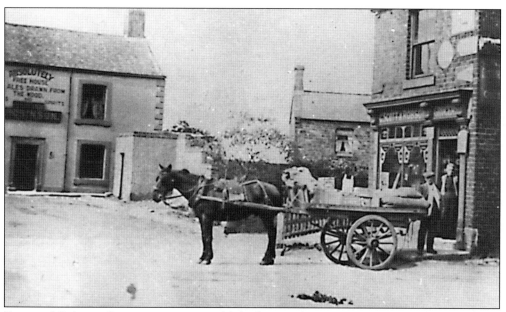

Scott and Robsons Grocery store was established at number six Percy Terrace, during the early 1900s. The owners, Mr and Mrs Scott are standing in the doorway, probably in the process of taking a delivery. Note the old Ship Inn and East Farm in the background.

Taken from the top of Percy Terrace in 1910, this shows another view of Scott & Robsons shop. The main entrance to the Black Horse Inn was via the wooden porch next door.

Front Street, Monkseaton, around 1908. The Black Horse Inn is to the extreme left, with the white fronted cottages of Coronation Row just beyond it. To the right, in the foreground, is the perimeter wall forming part of South West Farm, followed by Village Farm. The white cottage beyond it, was once the residence of Mr W. Brown, the village blacksmith.

In reality, the picturesque area known as Briar Dene was more a part of Whitley Bay than Monkseaton, but this scene, taken from a 1904 picture postcard, states otherwise!

Two
Farms, Fields and Inns

The Old Ship Inn, 1912. The Ship Inn was originally a farmhouse, built in 1688 by Thomas Mills, and it stood on the site of what is now the junction of Percy Terrace and Lyndhurst Road. It was first converted to a public house in 1790. The building was demolished in 1923, and rebuilt on a site slightly further to the west, near the end of Roseberry Terrace.

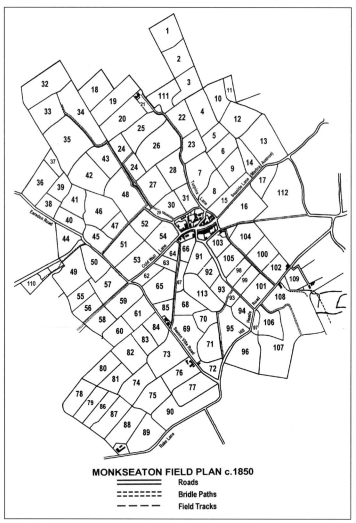

MONKSEATON FIELD PLAN c.1850

═══════	Roads
════════	Bridle Paths
─ ─ ─ ─	Field Tracks

The following plan is based on an old tithe map dated around 1850, and it shows the farmland and fields encircling Monkseaton Village. During this time, many of the fields were given names; the locations can be pinpointed by the numbers shown, to the farms that they relate to. The * indicates that these fields have no recorded name.

East Farm

1   Far Field
2   Whinney Lea
3   Starcher Stank
4   Well Field
5   Kerseys Killinghole (North)
6   Kerseys Killinghole (South)
7   Stephensons Close
8   High Pump Field
9   Low Pump Field

North East (Village Farm)

10   Middle Field
11   Clay Bank Close
12   South Middle Field
13   North Road Field
14   Farm Road Field
15   Brewery Field
16   South or Village Field
17   South Road Field

Red House Farm

18	*
19	Long Back Field
20	Long West Field
21	*
22	Near South Field
23	Far South Field

North Farm

24	North Field
25	North East Field
26	Middle Field
27	Hill Field
28	Sandy (Reans) Veins Field
29	West Town Field
30	Town Field
31	East Town Field

North West Farm

32	*
33	North Corn Pasture
34	Meadow Field (near & far Pickerlaw)
35	(Whitefields) South Corn Pasture
36	North Close
37	Restley Close
38	North West Field
39	North East Field
40	West Low Field
41	East Middle Field
42	Berris Hill (West Pasture)
43	Berris Hill (East Pasture)
44	Triangular Close
45	Tolls Close (Todds Close)
46	North Bog Field
47	Bog Foot (West Bog)
48	Bog Foot (East Bog), Berris Hill & Pickerlaw Hill
49	North Ridges, West Ridges (South) & Earsdon West Ridges
50	North Middle Ridges & West Ridges
51	North Ridges & New Ridge
52	North Town End Close & Town End Field Close
53	South Ridges & Well Ridges
54	Town End Field Close & Near Town End Close

West Farm

55	North West Close
56	South West Close
57	East or Road Field

South West Farm

58	*
59	*
60	*
61	*
62	Fatting Pasture
63	South Caseton
64	North Caseton
65	Low Close

Seatonville Farm

66	*
67	*
68	The Fleets
69	*
70	*
71	*
72	*
73	*
74	*
75	*
76	*
77	*

Burnt House Farm

78	*
79	*
80	*
81	*
82	*
83	*
84	*
85	*

Rake House Farm

86	*
87	*
88	*
89	*
90	*

South Farm

91	North Close
92	South North Close
93	Middle Close
94	South Close
95	Fox Holes Close
96	Ropesteads Field & Ropestead Close
97	*
98	North Brewery Close
99	South Brewery Close
100	Brickyard Close
101	Hill Head Close
102	Stackyard Close

Monkseaton (Bygate Farm)

103	North West Field
104	East Field
105	South West Field

Hill Heads Farm

106	Four Nooked Close
107	Middle Park Field
108	Quarry Head & The Old Quarries
109	West Hill Head

Dickies Holm (Blacksmiths Farm)

110	*

Miscellaneous

111	Shankeys Field
112	Whitley Nook
113	Chamberlains Meadow

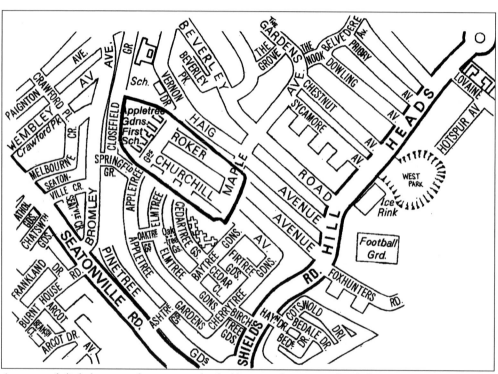

An area of slightly more than ten and a half acres of common land, known as Chamberlains Meadow, stood amongst the many fields in Monkseaton, and its location is superimposed on the modern map above. The first record of Chamberlains Meadow is taken from an old tithe map dating from the mid 1500s, when it was known that the land was farmed by the whole township of Monkseaton. During the 1700s and 1800s, it was used as common grazing land, and remained as such until the present houses were built. The origin of the name Chamberlains Meadow is unknown.

Monkseaton South West Farm, which stood on the corner of Front Street and Chapel Lane. The farm dates to the early 1700s, with the farmland covering an area of almost 244 acres. During March 1950, the farm buildings were altered and renovated in order to accommodate offices, a builder's merchant, and a showroom. In later years, the trees were removed, and the section facing onto Front Street was converted into a small supermarket.

South West Farm around 1960. The farm buildings which still exist, are accessible from Chapel Lane. The old farmyard is located behind the stone wall, and is now used for commercial purposes.

Looking east along Bygate Road, 1896; Bygate Farm can be seen in the distance. The cottages to the left are numbered 6, 8 and 10 Bygate Road, which have unusual wooden porches with Masonic symbols, in the form of a square and compasses above the doors. It has been speculated that the reason for these symbols was because at one time they were used as meeting places for Masonic Rituals, but this is thought to be highly improbable. It is more likely that the symbols were purely ornamental, or that the builders themselves may have had Masonic connections. In any event, the true reason has never been established.

This 1948 view of Bygate Road, shows Rock Cottage on the left, with the corner of Coronation Crescent in the background. Part of Bygate Farm, built in 1735, is visible to the right, and stands next to the junction with The Gardens. The last of the farm buildings were demolished in 1950. The Witchen trees growing in the centre of the road have stood there for many years, and are reputed to have been planted by farmers in the belief that they would keep any evil spirits away.

42

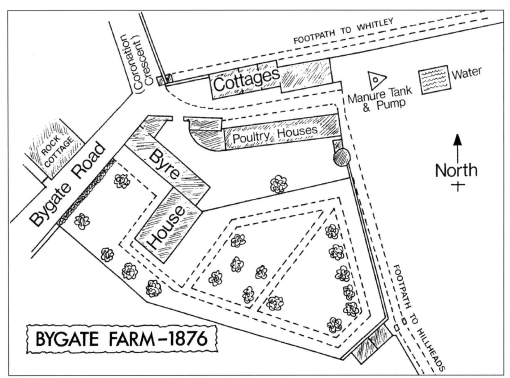

This 1876 plan shows the location of the area occupied by Bygate Farm.

This 1905 picture shows an unknown lady, standing at the front door of what is believed to be North Farm, on Front Street, Monkseaton. The buildings were later altered to accommodate a firm of builders merchants before demolition in 1986, to make way for a sheltered housing project.

Preparation work starts in 1986 for the demolition of Monkseaton North Farm buildings, latterly known as 'Coast Builders' Merchants'.

North Farm buildings have disappeared, and were by September 1986, replaced by Homeprior House sheltered housing project, shown here as it nears completion.

The new Ship Inn, Monkseaton, during construction work in 1922. The original Ship Inn is still standing to the extreme right.

A fireplace, carved with the date 1688, in one of the upper rooms of the original Ship Inn. Above the fireplace, in stucco, is the coat of arms of Charles II, with the Royal monogram 'CR', along with the Stuart motto 'Beati Pacifici', which means 'Blessed are the Peacemakers'. The coat of arms was removed and 'rescued' by several public-spirited citizens when the old inn was demolished in 1923. It was later presented to the town, and preserved in the Urban District Council Chambers at Whitley Bay.

The new Ship Inn was built for the Northumberland Brewery Company, (the then owners of Monkseaton Brewery), and was intended to replace the first inn of the same name. The inn is shown here, on completion in 1923. A plaque was erected above the door which reads: '1688, Ye Olde Ship Inn. Rebuilt 1923' Newcastle Breweries acquired the building from the Northumberland Brewery Company in 1934.

Part of Monkseaton North West Farm, included the building known as Monkseaton dairy farm, which is seen here under demolition in 1922. This building stood on the site of the present Ship Inn. Roseberry Terrace can be seen in the background.

The original Black Horse Inn, shortly before its demolition in 1936. The row of houses to the left is Percy Terrace.

A more familiar and recognisable Black Horse in 1952.

Monkseaton Brewery around 1900. Long before Monkseaton Brewery was built, the monks who inhabited the village, brewed ale which was often sold to travellers. Monkseaton Brewery was built in 1683 for Michael Turpin of Murton, and at the time it was the largest and most conspicuous building in Monkseaton, with whitewashed walls, a red pantiled roof and a tall chimney, which could be seen for many miles around. During this time, Michael Turpin bought a cottage, which stood immediately to the west of the brewery buildings. This cottage was later to become the first Monkseaton Arms. Turpin gave his name to the road that ran alongside the brewery towards Red House Farm, namely 'Turpins Lane'. The road was known by this name for many years, until in latter years it was renamed as Relton Terrace.

Over the years, the brewery changed hands many times. Three fires are recorded there, the first of which occurred on 9 March 1821, and totally destroyed the drying kiln along with sixty bolls of malt. The second fire occurred on 4 January 1849 when the malting and stables were burned down. Five of the six brewery horses perished, and were buried in Chamberlains Meadow (see p. 40). The third fire occurred in 1860, destroying part of the buildings containing much of the brewery machinery, however all of the damage was repaired.

The local farmers delivered grain to the brewery with a horse and cart, and along with the draymen, were usually rewarded with a 'horn' of ale before leaving. A horse-drawn dray would be loaded with barrels of ale at the side of the brewery, through a 'loading hole', which was a kind of dock formed so that the barrels could be run directly off the ground onto the cart or dray. Malt making was carried out on the upper floors.

During 1855, the brewery was in the possession of William Davison who resided at Monkseaton House, next door to the brewery. Two reservoirs were built in the rear garden of the house, in order to supply the brewery with water. There is a story that the brewery was once connected to Monkseaton House by a tunnel. In 1900, the brewery was taken over by the Northumberland Brewery Company, and sold by them to the Newcastle Breweries in 1934. Shortly afterwards, the brewery buildings and public house were demolished to make way for the present Monkseaton Arms.

The sheer scale and size of Monkseaton Brewery during the 1800s is depicted in this sketch.

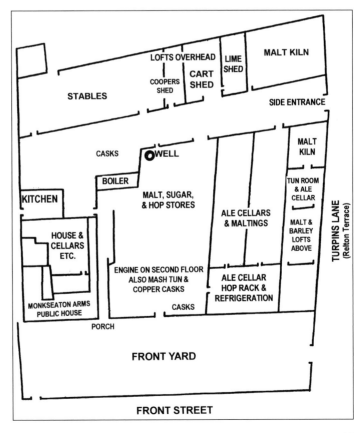

A ground floor plan of Monkseaton Brewery, dated 1879.

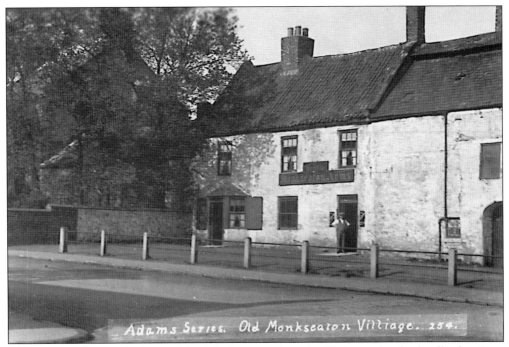

The man standing at the door of the Monkseaton Arms in 1920, may be the landlord waiting for some customers!

Two men, with their horse and cart seen outside Monkseaton Brewery in 1902.

In 1905, a young girl sits on the railings of a deserted Front Street, by the Monkseaton Arms.

Today the Monkseaton Arms is more affectionately known to the regulars as 'The Monkey'. This picture was taken in 1986, prior to the latest alterations. A part of the original brewery wall is still visible in the background beside the trees.

This small building, located between the Monkseaton Arms and Monkseaton House, was formerly used as a harness-room for the Monkseaton Brewery. When the brewery disappeared, it was taken over and run as a pet shop for a number of years by M. Blackbourn. It was then demolished in the 1960s to make way for a small bank branch, and was later converted into a shop.

This 1950 view of Rake Lane looks east towards the Foxhunters, and shows Rake House Farm, which stood towards the far south-westerly corner of Monkseaton Township. The house to the right has long since disappeared, but the gable end of the actual farmhouse, dates back to around 1660, and is visible on the left of the picture. Along with a good proportion of its land, the farmhouse still remains to this day. It is situated virtually opposite the North Tyneside General Hospital.

Seatonville Road, looking north from the Foxhunters in 1924. The houses and buildings are all part of Seaton Ville Farm, and date back as far as 1625. Of the two terraced farm cottages shown to the right of the picture, the one nearest the road was demolished during the 1920s to facilitate the widening of Seatonville Road. In later years, as the farm fell into disuse, the buildings on the left were demolished and replaced by the houses that are numbered 129 to 147 Seatonville Road. These houses were built on the site of the farm outbuildings and stackyard; and Monkseaton High School is built on the land to the rear.

Burnt House Farm was built around 1700, and covered an area of over one hundred and twelve acres of land. The actual farmhouse stood on Seatonville Road, at the junction with what is now Bromley Avenue. In earlier times, the farm was joined to Monkseaton Village by a pathway, which followed the course of the present Bromley Avenue, through a field, which was known as 'The Fleets'. In 1929, shortly after this photograph was taken, the farm buildings were demolished, and replaced with houses. Nos 64, 66 and 68 Seatonville Road, now occupy this site.

Seatonville Road was once a narrow country lane until widening work commenced in 1925. This view looks south towards the Foxhunters in 1924, from what is now the junction with Bromley Avenue. Burnt House Farm buildings are to the left with Seaton Ville Farm visible in the distance, behind the trees.

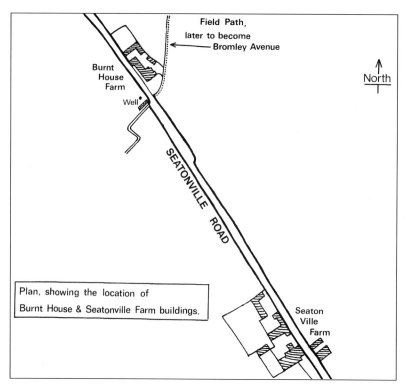

This plan shows Seatonville Road, indicating the positions of both Burnt House, and Seaton Ville Farms.

Three
Monkseaton Outskirts

The old Monkseaton Railway Station, referred to as Whitley Station, was built in 1859. The station and tracks ran in front of Osborne Gardens. By 1915, the railway track had been re-aligned and moved to its present position, further to the west. A road bridge was built and the new Monkseaton Station was opened. These buildings were demolished during the 1920s, and the area was landscaped to create Souter Park.

A steam shovel clears a cutting for re-alignment of the track, during construction work for the new Monkseaton Railway Station, 1883.

Whitley (Monkseaton) Station around 1900. Marine Avenue crosses the railway lines at the level crossing gates. The main station buildings can be seen to the right, whilst the signal box stood to the left.

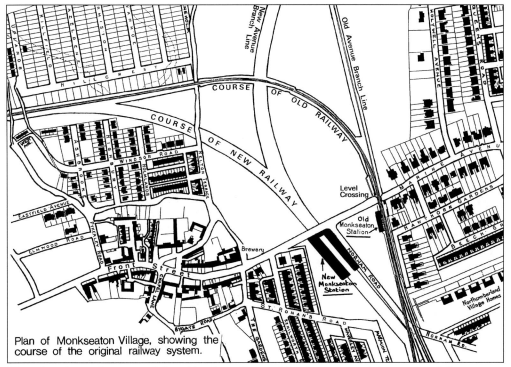

Plan of Monkseaton Village, showing the course of the original railway system.

This plan shows the route of the old railway line at Monkseaton, and the course of the new re-aligned track, which was completed in 1915.

The north platform of Monkseaton Station in 1950.

An electric train waits for passengers at Monkseaton Station in 1952.

During 1877, it was felt that there was a need to establish an institution for the reception and training of little girls who were either orphans or destitute. In 1879, the Duke of Northumberland provided a site on which to build the village homes, and the construction costs were made possible by a number of local wealthy benefactors. Building work commenced in 1879, and the homes were completed by 1908. The homes remained in use until the 1970s, when the site was taken over to be converted into a modern housing area, and was renamed 'Village Court'. All of the original houses remain, having been modernised to accommodate individual private housing needs. The house in the foreground is now No. 96 Village Court.

A leisurely bowling match in progress at Souter Park during the 1940s. The park was named after Councillor C.W. Souter, who led the negotiations with the North Eastern Railway Company to develop the land, following the relocation and demolition of the former railway station which stood on the site.

Prior to the houses being built on Marine Avenue, the street was simply known as 'Seaside Lane'. This view looks west towards Monkseaton. In the distance the railway signals can be seen at the point where the railway lines crossed the road, prior to the construction of the present Monkseaton Station and road-bridge.

These impressive villas, built during the 1890s are Nos 68-88 Marine Avenue. This picture was taken in 1905.

Marine Avenue, at the junction with Holywell Avenue in 1905.

MARINE AVENUE, MONKSEATON. (337)

This 1920s view looks east along Marine Avenue towards the seafront, from the junction with Ilfracombe Gardens and Park View. The large house in the left foreground is No. 52 Marine Avenue. Barely visible, but standing in the distance at the corner of Park Road, are a group of houses, which over the years were converted into what are now more familiar as shops and amusement arcades.

Looking towards the seafront, around 1905. It is apparent that the houses on the north side of Marine Avenue had not yet been constructed; however, on the opposite side of the road, the substantial terraced houses, with attic rooms, look very impressive.

This view of Ilfracombe Gardens was taken around 1918, and looks south towards Marine Avenue, with some of the buildings on Park View visible in the far distance. Kew Gardens is the junction just off the photograph, to the immediate right. The second block of houses are beyond the junction with Eastbourne Gardens, most of which have now been converted into shops. The people standing at the front door of No. 27 Ilfracombe Gardens seem to be engrossed in conversation, whilst the two children in the centre happily take a stroll.

A residential part of Ilfracombe Gardens, looking south from the junction with Bournemouth Gardens, during the 1930s. The house on the left is No. 108 Ilfracombe Gardens, which was later converted into a shop.

A cobbled Eastbourne Gardens, as seen from the junction with Ilfracombe Gardens, around 1912. The shop to the right bears a sign, 'Bygate Dairy Stores'. It has long since disappeared, having been bricked up to form part of the building on the corner. Immediately across the lane, another shop is visible to the left, beyond which the gable end of No. 28 Bideford Gardens can be seen.

Eastbourne Gardens, 1921, looking towards the Seafront from near the junction with Bideford Gardens. The old Links Bandstand can be seen at the end of the street.

In earlier years, Windsor Gardens was one of the many older streets in Monkseaton and Whitley that were laid out with cobblestones. This picture was taken during 1910 at the junction with Queens Road. The large house on the right corner is number one Windsor Gardens.

A cyclist on his delivery bicycle during the 1920s, takes a rest to pose for this photograph, taken on Queens Road, at the junction with Windsor Gardens, Monkseaton. The house to the immediate right has been identified as No. 44 Queens Road. The view looks north towards Monkseaton Drive.

Kings Road, looking west around 1921. An unusual looking delivery tricycle standing outside of Nos 22 and 24, probably making a delivery of fresh cream, as there appears to be a small churn attached to the front carrier.

A quiet, residential Balmoral Gardens, around 1920. The large three storey house on the corner, is actually No. 4 Queens Road.

The row of shops which stand at the northern end of Seatonville Road were built during the early 1930s. Tennants chemist shop incorporated West Monkseaton post office, the pillar-box of which can be seen standing opposite. Whites Grocery shop next door is followed by G.D Ewans Butchers, an old established local business, which still trades to this day. In this photograph, taken during the mid 1930s, a sign is visible at the end of the row of shops, advertising the new houses for sale as West Farm Estate.

Oaktree Gardens, around 1954. These shops were centrally placed on Seatonville council estate in order to serve the surrounding community. Well-designed and functional flats with a balcony were incorporated above the shops.

In this 1950s picture, these new council houses are at the corner of Pinetree Gardens and Shields Road. Seatonville Road, in the foreground has since been altered and widened to accommodate what is better known locally as the 'Foxhunters Roundabout'

During the early 1920s, George Dawson Ewen established a butcher's shop in Coronation Crescent, Monkseaton. The business was a success, and a second shop opened during the 1930s at No. 7 Seatonville Road, West Monkseaton. His nephew, John Ewen (pictured on the left) eventually took over the business, and is seen here with Vic Homer, a long serving staff member at the Seatonville Road premises around 1960. John Ewen died in 1997, but the business still remains with the family, and is now run by the great nephew of the founder – John Dawson Ewen.

This advertisement is dated 1936, and West Farm Estate refers to the semi-detached houses built between Canberra Avenue and Athol Gardens during this time. With prices starting from £495, it is amazing to think how much they are selling for now! Although named 'West Farm Estate', there must have been some confusion over the name of the area on which it was built, as the land concerned actually belonged to South Farm! The name probably never mattered anyway, as it was never known as an 'estate' in the conventional sense of the word. The land belonging to West Farm stood adjacent, and to the west of what is now Cauldwell Avenue.

68

The old Co-operative store, which has barely changed in appearance over the years, stood on the corner of Seatonville Road and Canberra Avenue. When the Co-op closed down in the 1960s, the butchery department around the corner was converted into a post office and the main shop became a newsagents.

The Classic Cinema was originally built during the 1930s as 'The Regal', and stood at the junction of Cauldwell Lane and Seatonville Road. As the popularity of home video and multiplex entertainment centres grew, the cinema was forced out of business, and finally closed its doors in 1999.

As the housing development progressed in the West Monkseaton area, the London and North Eastern Railway decided to build a new station between Monkseaton and Backworth, and as a result West Monkseaton Station was opened on 20th March 1933.

Marine Avenue, 1905.

Four
Hillheads

A quiet Shields Road, Hillheads Estate, around 1950, showing Birchtree Gardens Junction on the left, with Haydon Drive to the right. The newly-built rows of council houses still remain, and the young saplings have now grown into mature trees.

Richard Heckels Nesbit was born at Cramlington in 1830. In 1857 he travelled abroad where he made his fortune working in the goldfields of Australia and New Zealand. On returning to England in 1867, he married a Miss Mary Jobling. Shortly after, moving to Whitley in 1875, he purchased Bygate Farm in Monkseaton and set up a brickworks on land at Hill Heads, on the western edge of the limestone quarry at Marden. Richard served on Whitley Urban District Council for twenty years, and together with Alfred Styan, they became pioneer builders in Whitley. They were responsible for most of the construction of Albany Gardens, Clarence Crescent, Edwards Road, the Esplanade, Laburnum Avenue, Station Road and Mafeking Street (later re-named Fern Avenue). By 1889, the brickworks at Hill Heads were exhausted, so Nesbit ceased operations, and landscaped the entire area in order to create an area known as West Park. He died there on 28th March 1911, aged eighty-one. He was interred at St Pauls church, Whitley Bay.

This picture is taken from a painting by an unknown artist. The trees in the background show the line of the present day Hillheads Road.

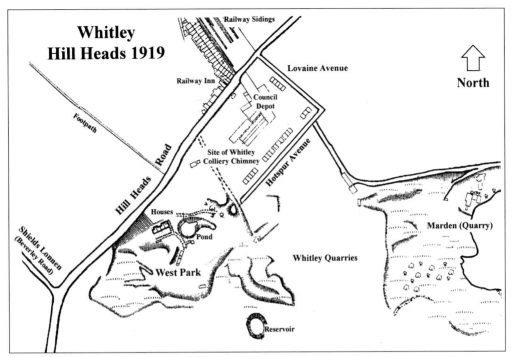

A map of Whitley Hill Heads, dated 1919.

A row of four cottages, constructed in West Park during the time that Nesbits Brickworks were in operation. The area had been landscaped at the time that Richard Heckles Nesbit posed for this photograph, with his pony and trap, taken outside the front of his residence at No. 1 West Park, during the early 1900s. The woman with him, is probably his wife, Mary Jobling.

The area of land adjacent to the ice rink at Hillheads, now used as a cricket and recreation field, is known as West Park. When Richard Heckels Nesbit died in 1911, West Park was sold to Mr George Steel, a florist and nurseryman from Park View, Whitley Bay. George Steel utilised the area as market gardens where he built stables and made a number of improvements to the land. West Park at this time was a deep quarry with steep sides, approximately ninety feet below the level of the adjacent Hill Heads Road. There were one hundred and thirty-four wood-fronted clay steps descending from the main road into the quarry, terminating at the rear of the row of houses at the bottom. George Steel and his family took up residence in Nesbits former house at No. 1 West Park, which is the end house on the right. He rented the remaining three houses out. No. 2 was let to a family called Glendinning, and Nos 3 and 4 to a family called Turner. George owned West Park until 1924, when Whitley Urban District Council placed a compulsory purchase order on the land, forcing him to move out shortly afterwards. This picture was taken about 1912, from a position slightly to the north east of where the present ice rink stands. In the background, the steeple of St Pauls church can be seen to the extreme right. Also visible is the tall chimney and winding shaft from the old Whitley Colliery. These were located in what became the Urban District Council Yard, virtually opposite the site of what is now the present Railway Inn. The rows of houses, visible towards the centre of the picture are Kenilworth Road, and Waverley Avenue.

When the compulsory purchase order on West Park took effect in 1924, the cottages were razed to the ground and the council began infilling the land with thousands of tons of earth and rubble, commencing at the western edge of the land. By 1931, controlled refuse tipping was also in progress. Eventually, the original ninety feet deep quarry/park was raised to its present level, grassed over and landscaped to become what is now West Park cricket field. The houses in the background form part of Hillheads Road which runs left to right. The street directly behind the marker pole, near the centre of the picture, is Chestnut Avenue.

West Park, April 2000. This picture was taken from exactly the same place as the 1926 photograph (opposite). There is a vast difference from the picturesque park of 1912, and the rubbish tip of 1931.

Joseph William Steel was the son of George Steel. He was born in 1884 at Heatherslaw, Northumberland, and on moving to Whitley Bay in 1901 with his father, he resided for a short period at No. 288 Whitley Road. In 1911, when his father purchased West Park, at Hill Heads, he married and moved into one of the cottages there. Along with his brother, Richard, he ran the market gardens at Park View, and at West Park, Hill Heads. He died on 5th November 1928 at the age of forty-four.

This view of West Park is dated sometime between 1900 and 1911 when it was still in the possession of Richard Heckels Nesbit. When George Steel took over the land, many of the old outbuildings were demolished to make way for new stables and greenhouses.

George Steel was born in 1849, at Barmoor Castle, Northumberland. He first established a business at Heatherslaw and Etal Village, Northumberland, before moving with his family to Whitley Bay in 1901, where he set up a market garden and florists on Park View, which for many years were known as Steels Gardens. With his two sons, Richard and Joseph, he ran the gardens, which stood on the site now occupied by shops, opposite St Pauls church. By 1911, the nurseries had expanded, and so George Steel purchased West Park, at Hill Heads from Richard Heckels Nesbit. George Steel died in 1937.

Richard Steel, the son of George Steel, who along with his brother, Joseph William, ran Steel's market gardens at Whitley Bay and Hill Heads.

The old Whitley Colliery chimney was a landmark at Hill Heads for many years and stood within the confines of Whitley council yard. It was demolished in 1953.

The Railway Inn, around 1919. Originally known as the Crown & Thistle during the early 1800s, it was later renamed as the Railway Inn, presumably having derived the name from Monkseaton Railway Station sidings, which stood towards the rear of the building. John Dawson, of Whitley Bay ran the pub, which stood on the same site as the present building of the same name. He married an Esther Emerson, of Wearhead, and they are seen here standing under the signboard at the front doorway. John Dawson died at the pub aged seventy-four, on 6 May 1924, followed by Esther on 8 January 1928, aged seventy-seven.

The new and more familiar Railway Inn was built on the site of the previous building of the same name. This picture is dated 1982.

Hill Heads Farm, taken from a sketch dated 1913. The old Whitley Colliery chimney and winding shaft is visible behind the stables.

For a period of 200 years, from the mid-1600s, magnesium limestone was quarried at Marden and Hill Heads. Large quantities of this stone were transported via a waggon-way, to be shipped abroad from loading staithes at North Shields. When the limestone workings ceased, Marden Reservoir was formed, and overseen by the North Shields and Tynemouth Water Company. The cottages opposite were called 'New Whitley', but locally, they were more colourfully known as 'Fiddler's Green'. Along with the stone tower to the left of the picture, they were demolished in the mid 1960s. In 1977, the area was landscaped to form what is now a wildlife sanctuary, called Marden Park.

The Quarry Tower, Marden, as seen from the inside of the quarry. The stone tower, which stood on Marden Road for many years, was originally built as offices, and may also have been used as a powder and explosives store. The tower was a landmark for many years, until it was demolished in 1965. The painting dates from around 1900, but the name of the artist is unknown.

The Broadway, as seen from Marden Tower, during the early 1920s. The view along this once winding road looks south towards Tynemouth, and Marden Farm can be seen in the distance. The area of land to the left is now occupied by housing.

The original Quarry Inn dates from about 1854, and stood at the south eastern extremity of Hill Heads, at its boundary with Marden. This view, dated 1914, looks north along the path of the old Broadway, and shows the original Quarry Inn, which stood at what is now the entrance to Marden Park. When the Broadway was straightened during the early 1920s, the Quarry Inn was demolished, and rebuilt on the opposite side of the new road. However this section of the Broadway remained, and it now serves as an access road to feed Marden Farm Estate.

A more familiar Quarry Inn, 1982.

This painting of Marden Farm, and the old Quarry Inn dates to around 1912. The name of the artist is unknown.

Five
Earsdon and Holywell Dene

Earsdon Village, from Earsdon Road, Shiremoor in 1904.

Earsdon Village lies to the north of Monkseaton on rising ground, and derives its name from the old English name of Erdes-dun, (the word 'dun' meaning a hill). This eventually changed to Earsdon, by which name it is better known as today. At one time, Earsdon Village supported four public houses, those being the Red Lion, the Cannon, The Phoenix, and the lesser-known Plough Inn. The lime-washed building towards the right is the old Phoenix Inn, which closed its doors as a public house in 1971. This early picture is dated 1874 and shows a crowd of villagers gathered outside the post office.

A local landmark for miles around is St Albans church built in 1837, but its origins, along with Earsdon, date back to the thirteenth century, when the site was occupied by a previous place of worship. In 1862, an extension was made to the north side of the churchyard to inter 204 bodies, recovered from the nearby New Hartley Colliery, following a catastrophic mining disaster during this year. The graves took up an area of over an acre of land.

84

A granite obelisk and memorial erected in St Albans churchyard, lists the names of the 204 men and boys who perished in the New Hartley Colliery mining disaster of 1862.

Looking south along Front Street, Earsdon around 1920. The single storey stone building to the right of the picture is the old smithy, which has since undergone a number of changes, and has now been converted into a house.

A view of Earsdon in 1904, looking west into the village. The second Primitive Methodist chapel, built in 1886, can be seen to the right, and the white fronted building remembered by many people, is the old Phoenix Inn. The group of cottages between them, and behind the trees are 'Taylors Cottages', named after Hugh Taylor, a local landowner who opened Earsdon Colliery in 1824.

Bank Top, Earsdon Village in 1902, looking towards Holywell. The very first Red Lion Pub stood here, and is the building with the cart standing outside.

Earsdon Village around 1912, as seen from the corner of Garden Terrace. The horse and cart in the background wait patiently outside of what was once the general dealers store and post office.

Stewarts General Dealers store, and the old post office, Earsdon Village in 1916. The shop and post office have long since disappeared, and the building has since been converted into residential houses.

A very rural Earsdon Village, on a summers day in 1930.

In 1730, two adjoining cottages were built on Hartley Lane, Earsdon, to house the clerks who managed Lord Delavals estates, and as a result, they were colourfully referred to as 'Clarks House'. These houses were vacated in 1815, and taken over by a Quaker family who made several alterations and modified the buildings to establish a dairy farm. In 1896, the farm was converted into a public house, which was named the Beehive. This painting is dated 1892, when the house was still in use as a farm.

A painting of the Beehive Inn, by F. Dallas in 1896 – the year it first opened as a public house. The plaque above the door shows that the name of the first licensee was James Linfoot. Most of the ales supplied to the pub at this time were delivered from Monkseaton Brewery. A tall pole stood to the rear of the pub, and during the First and Second World War, a flag was raised to full mast indicating to the residents of the nearby villages of Wellfield, Earsdon, Holywell and Old Hartley, that an ample supply of ales were available! In 1986, the Beehive became a listed building.

For many years, Holywell Dene has been a local beauty spot. In 1880, a local writer. William Weaver Tomlinson, wrote: 'Holywell Dene is a charming place for a picnic. It may be reached through pleasant paths through the fields from Whitley and Monkseaton. The Seaton Burn flows through the dene, and in the upper part, especially near the mill-dam, where the branches of lofty trees over-arch it, forms some exquisite little pictures of sylvan loveliness. An excellent tea is supplied to the visitor at the Crow Hall Farm, which stands about the left bank of the dene, and is reached by a broad and shady path leading from the wooden bridge over the stream'.

Holywell Dene is situated just over a mile from both Monkseaton and Earsdon Villages, just off Hartley Lane, near to the Beehive Inn. This tranquil view of the dene, complete with a picnic party, is dated 1919.

A summers day stroll in Holywell Dene, 1908.

Seaton Lodge, seen here, is situated at the end of Holywell Dene, and in 1903, these children seem to be quite content, relaxing next to the stream.

Seaton Lodge Farm sits higher on the hillside, whilst Seaton Lodge and the Old Mill gently bask by the stream at the northernmost end of Holywell Dene.

Starlight Castle, Holywell Dene 1906. At one time, the Delavals were a prominent family of nobility in the area. This small castle is reputed to have been built in a day in order to provide accommodation for a dignified lady visitor from London, thus winning, for one of the Delavals, a one hundred guinea wager.

Six
Murton and New York

The name of Murton is derived from Moor Town, which in 1825 was described as a village containing fifty-seven houses, three public houses, and five hundred and sixty-three inhabitants, most of which were employed in the nearby coal mines. This picture taken in 1905, from Well Lane shows the only remaining and recognisable building left in the village, the Robin Hood Inn, which is almost hidden from sight behind the farmsteads. The inn still thrives, but sadly, as progress moves forward, all of the old cottages and surrounding farm buildings have long since disappeared.

Murton House stands next to what is commonly referred to as 'Jacksons Farm', on Rake Lane, near the junction with New York Road. The house still exists today. This picture was taken in 1905.

Moor Cottage, in 1906. The exact location of this cottage has not been established, but it is believed to have stood on Murton Lane, between the Wheatsheaf Inn and Murton Village.

New York Road, looking east in 1905. The building to the immediate left is J&B Millers Cash Dividend Store, beyond which is the Dun Cow Public House. Both these buildings remain to this day.

This picture, dated 1911, shows New York Schools, which were built in 1874. The schools, remembered by many people, stood on New York Road, at the western end of Brookland Terrace, the terraced houses of which can be seen in the distance.

Rose Cottage and Woodbine House in 1905. This view is taken from the end of what used to be part of Middle Engine Lane. As redevelopment of the area progressed, the houses were demolished, and the roads were widened and renamed. However the small building to the right, which was the village blacksmiths shop known as the Robin Hood Forge, remained. New York Road runs from left to right in front of the facing house and forge, and the lane leading to Murton Village is directly ahead.